Easy Lie Detection

By

Mark Menefee

Copyright © 2012 Mark Menefee

All rights reserved.

ISBN-13: 978-1479363483
ISBN-10: 1479363480

No part of this publication may be copied or reproduced in any format, by any means, electronic or otherwise, without prior written consent from the copyright owner and publisher of this book.

## Table of Contents

Introduction
- Techniques for Detecting Deception
- Psychological Aspects of Interviewing
- The Subject

Verbal Content Analysis
- The Interview
- Obtain the "Initial" version of the story
- Language Indicators of Deception
- Rules for the Detailed Interview
- Closing the interview

Non-verbal Behavior Analysis (NBA)
- The Interview
- NON-VERBAL BEHAVIOR ANALYSIS Indicators

Summary

Introduction

Can you really tell if someone is lying? The answer is a qualified "YES." If the techniques disclosed here are correctly applied, lying or deception can be detected approximately 80% of the time. To illustrate this please review the following illustrated scenarios. Can you tell me if the people are being truthful? No, well we will review these scenarios again in the last chapter and by then you should be able to tell if the subjects are being deceptive. Please take a moment to make a decision for each scenario. Don't just guess. If you can't articulate why you answered as you did, please wait until you finish reading the book to answer. Don't jump ahead or you will miss many of the nuances that will help you to spot if there is any deception.

## Techniques for Detecting Deception

There is lying and there is deception. Why do I make this distinction? Because, most of the time people deceive you with partial truths and misdirection, instead of outright lies. This is true in business dealings, criminal investigations, civil investigations, and personal matters. Generally, people prefer **not** to lie, as it is quite stressful. However, if a subject misleads you with the truth it is not nearly as stressful. Remember the old adage, "If you tell the truth you don't have to remember what you said." Much of the information given here relates to detecting deception, which is a more common way to cover up or hide the truth.

There are two primary systems for detecting deception without the use of a polygraph, Non-Verbal Behavior Analysis and Verbal Content

Analysis. Non-Verbal Behavior Analysis is the study of human movement as it relates to detecting deception, body language. Studies have identified specific movement indicators and there relation to the subject's emotions or state of mind regarding truthfulness. An overview of these movements and how to interpret them are included. Verbal Content Analysis relies on the specific spoken verbal word. Verbal Content Analysis evaluates both what was said and how it was said. I personally lean more heavily on Verbal Content Analysis because it is easier to use in practice, but I do watch for Non-Verbal Behavior Analysis indicators. Studies have shown using the two techniques together can significantly increase the reliability of the results. One study demonstrated that when interviewers combined what was said, with how it was said, along with the non-verbal behavior cues the truthfulness of a subject could be determined over 80% of the time. Be aware that high stakes lies are more easily detected than low stake lies. The level of risk to the subject correlates directly to the ability to detect the subject's lies.

Generally, I will describe how the techniques are used by investigators, but will also try to provide a discussion of how the general public can utilize the same techniques. Learning to effectively detect deception and lies can save you thousands, if not tens of thousands, of dollars and can help you to protect you and your family. These techniques require practice and concentration. **Unintended conflicts, particularly with family members, can occur if these techniques are not used judiciously.**

The author assumes no responsibility or liability for the application or mis-application of these techniques. Individual responses may vary based on cultural and personal norms. Additionally, ability to accurately detect the truth or a lie depends significantly on the ability of the interviewer. The totality of the circumstances and the information gathered must be used in determining deception. The following is an example of how assuming these rules are hard and fast can mislead you as to whether the subject is telling the truth.

The use of the phrase, "I swear to God," by an individual being interviewed is almost always indicative of deception. However, if the subject uses this term often, and in many instances, it is more probably a cultural norm. For both Non-Verbal Behavior Analysis and Verbal Content Analysis you need to establish a base line to be effective. A base line is an observation of the subject's physical and verbal patterns to establish what is normal for the subject. **This is critical for the use of both techniques.**

## Psychological Aspects of Interviewing

The following is a partial list of statements that have been proven to be accurate about humans and their responses to being interviewed or interrogated. There are some real nuggets here so don't just skim over them. This primarily relates to interviews and interrogations conducted by law enforcement personnel, but aspects of it do transfer to using the same techniques in your personal life. The interview or information gathering must come first. Gather all of the information you believe you can gather from the subject first. Move to an interrogation or accusatory mode only after you have gathered all necessary information, if appropriate.

**Innocent people do not confess.** (This presumes a legally conducted interview and interrogation where a subject is not placed under physical or mental duress such as threats.)

**Guilty subjects deny in specifics, innocent subjects deny inclusively.** (Read this statement again and remember it. It will help you tremendously if applied consistently to Verbal Content Analysis.)

**Listen to exactly what was said, not what you think was said.** (Your mind tends to fill in the blanks or missing information, don't.)

**Behavior indicators observed in clusters are more reliable than a single indicator.**

**You generally cannot insult a guilty person.** (It is almost impossible to make a guilty person mad to the point where they will get up and leave an interview. If you can make them mad, it will generally only be for a moment and then they will calm down. Guilty people feel an extreme need to maintain their calm so that they do not make a mistake in the interview.)

**Seventy-Five percent of guilty people will confess when interviewed and interrogated properly.**

**Non-verbal Behavior is responsible for almost half of the total communication.** (Body Language tells us a lot.)

**The interviewer's attitude and behavior has a significant influence on the subject being interviewed.** (This cannot be stressed enough. The interviewer must maintain a calm, non-judgmental demeanor that communicates understanding and trust.)

**The subject's behavior symptoms will become more dramatic as their anxiety level is increased.** (The higher the stakes, the greater the effect on the subject's behavior. The more the suspect has to lose, the greater their anxiety level and the more symptoms they will exhibit. The anxiety increases around the critical questions.)

**Verbal responses may contradict non-verbal indicators.** (Watch closely. This is a key indicator. The subject states "NO" to a question while nodding his head "YES'.)

**Behavior indicators become more reliable as the intelligence level of the subject increases.** (Note this is intelligence level not necessarily education level, although there may well be a correlation between the two.)

## The Subject

Generally you can divide the population into three groups for purposes of interviews and interrogations.

Logical – These individuals respond to the logic you present to them that the evidence shows them to be guilty. The evidence does not necessarily need to be to a level that a court expects, but only to a level that the subjects clearly believes indicates that he is lying or guilty. While it is a slippery slope, the courts have generally held that it is acceptable to lie to a suspect to gain a confession. This may be your only option to obtain a confession from this type of suspect if you do not have adequate evidence. Exercise caution when using deception to obtain a confession. Recent cases show that courts are more closely examining the reasonableness of the deception. A critical consideration is to be careful that you do not present a fact that the subject knows is a lie. If this happens you generally lose any chance of obtaining a confession through this technique.

Emotional – These individuals respond primarily on the emotional level and will tell you the truth if you can provide them the emotional support that allows them to rationalize their behavior. Just what does that mean? You have to indicate an understanding of why the subject took the action in question and that you or someone else might have taken a similar action. You may even have to indicate that the victim asked for it or that the victim was somehow at fault. The subject needs to be able to rationalize in their mind that their action was justified, even if they know it was not. While you may find this repulsive, sometimes it is the only way to obtain a confession where your evidence is weak.

Pathological – These people have no moral sense that what they have done is wrong. If you get a true pathological personality, which is fairly rare, you may never get to the truth. Career criminals will sometimes exhibit similar characteristics, but can often be maneuvered into telling the truth. Certain cultures and nationalities may also display this trait for certain crimes that would not be considered crimes in their native country or culture. Where there is an indication that the action would be acceptable in their country or culture, go back to the techniques for the emotional subject. Help them to rationalize their behavior based on their culture.

# Verbal Content Analysis

**THE TRUTH IS NOT THE TRUTH, WHEN IT MISLEADS US.**

There is the truth of what was said, and there is the whole truth. People will often make a statement that is completely true. However, that true statement will mislead you to an incorrect conclusion. Our minds fill in many of the blanks that are left unsaid, often incorrectly.

The specific language people use in telling their story is critical to detecting deception or lies.

But how do we get people to talk.

**We don't always know why people talk, but they do.**

**The more you expect the person to talk, the more the individual will talk.**

**People are afraid to ask questions, but they are not afraid to answer them.**

I can't emphasize the truth in these three statements enough. To demonstrate this, I want you to try an experiment next time you are in a restaurant. After the initial contact with the wait person ask them any number of simple questions. Where are you from? Are you going to school here? Where is your accent from? Ask any question that would indicate an interest in the person. Generally one question will suffice, but you may need a follow up question or two. Almost always they will tell you where they are from and as much of their life story as they can in the time available. People like to talk about themselves. If you ask them a question about themselves, and indicate an interest in them, it provides them an acceptable opportunity to talk about themselves. This one fact, has actually helped me to become more adept socially. We as a society are generally reticent, or afraid to ask people questions. If you start asking people about themselves, and just listen, they will think you are a wonderful conversationalist.

## The Interview

When conducting an interview using Verbal Content Analysis we want the interview to seem as non-confrontational as possible. Remember this is an interview to gather facts, not an interrogation, which is accusatory in nature. If you become accusatory in tone in the interview process, it will negatively affect your ability to document the full story. Documenting the original story is critical. If at all possible the interview should be recorded. There are several reasons.

1. If there is any possibility of legal action, criminal or civil, you will want the recording to corroborate the statements made in the interview. Without a recording it will simply be a he said, she said, argument. If you anticipate legal action I suggest you review evidentiary procedures for recordings. At a minimum you will need to do the following if you make a recording: secure the recording; be able to testify to the authenticity of the recording; and be able to testify that it has not been modified. If you can meet those standards you will probably be okay on getting it admitted into evidence.

2. You will want to go back over the recording for information and verbal cues that you missed during the interview. It is almost impossible to catch everything during the interview because you

will often have to formulate the next question. While you want a list of questions to make sure you cover everything, you have to pay sufficient attention to follow up on information discovered in the course of the interview. I have seen investigators loose valuable information because they stuck strictly to their list of questions and did not follow-up on the subject's responses. If you have the time and inclination, it is worth transcribing the interview to make analysis easier.

3. The final reason is to learn from your errors in the interview. I have never listened to one of my interviews where I did not hear something that I realized I should have followed-up on with additional questions. Often I was able to follow up with additional questions later because the original interview was not of an accusatory nature. A good way to end an interview is to ask the subject if you can contact them later if you have additional questions.

## Obtain the "Initial" version of the story

Obtaining the "initial" version of the story is critical to Verbal Content Analysis. The "Initial" version of the story is the story told as the subject chooses to tell it with minimal guidance and suggestion by the interviewer or third parties. Ask open ended general questions that encourage a person to go into a narration of events. Avoid questions which can be answered with a yes or no. A "tell me" statement from the interviewer can be quite effective, "Tell me what happened that night." Or "What can you tell me about last night?"

The interviewer should only be asking questions about 5% of the time. 95% of the time should be the subject responding to questions. If the time share is much different than this, the interviewer is probably becoming the interviewed.

If given the opportunity, the subject will tell the truth 90% of the time in response to an open ended question or "tell me" statement. Nearly always what the subject says will be true in response to this type question. All of the statement may be true, but what was omitted may lead the interviewer to the wrong conclusion. Remember there is the whole truth, and the truth of what is being said. If they do not say it, don't assume the fact in question. Be careful that you are hearing what was said, not what you expected to be said. We all tend to breeze through what was said because our brain tends to fill in the blanks. You can't do that if you wish to detect deception. You must listen to every word that was said and **never assume what was not said.**

Note: The first two problems are with the question. *First this is a double question that helps the subject provide a specific true response that will probably lead to an incorrect assumption by an*

interviewer. **Remember liars lie specifically**. However, the bigger problem is this is a close ended question. A far better question would have been a "tell me" statement. "Tell me where you were last night." That would be the first in a series of tell me statements to make sure we covered the full time period in question, who she saw, who she met with, what she did. Basically all of your what, when, why, where, and how questions need to be covered.

Second the response did not indicate that she did not have dinner with John last night. You cannot assume that they did not have dinner last night at a different location.

Note: The response still does not indicate that she did not see John last night. Very specific statements such as these should elicit further questions from you. **Remember liars lie specifically**. Both statements could be true and she still could have met with John last night. Also please note that both of these questions could be answered with a simple "no." An honest person would most probably have just answered "no."

An oral recitation of a story is not a chronology or reality. It is only what the person has decided to tell us. Everyone has a spell check that edits a story they are telling. This occurs even when a subject is not trying to be deceptive. The subject will make a decision either intentionally or unintentionally what is import to tell.

There are two stories within the story or narration a subject provides.

**1. The sequence of events.** The sequence of events is most easily controlled by the subject.

**2. The language used in telling the story.** The subject is generally not aware of the language they use and it is almost impossible to control. There are many verbal cues in this language that can help us determine if a subject is being deceptive.

Studies reflect that 28 % of deceptive subjects will make a detectable admission at some point during their initial story.

Detecting deception during the "initial" version.

1. Shortest way to give a sentence is usually the best! As illustrated above an honest subject would have just answered "No" to the closed question. Long rambling stories are indicative of a problem.

2. Every word the person says has meaning! We do not condense!

3.What the subject did not say also has significant meaning! If the subject hasn't said something happened, it didn't happen. We do not fill in the blanks! We do not assume!

## THE EDITING PROCESS
Subject decides what to tell – Regardless of whether the subject is a witness or suspect, they will condense the story down to what they think is important. They are **not** going to give you every detail to start with. It is up to you to listen to the story and identify areas where information has probably been left out and help discover that information. This is true in a formal interview or in personal conversations where a simple question is asked, such as, "How was the fishing trip?"

Personal verbal patterns – Individuals have personal characteristics about how they tell a story. Be aware of these characteristics if you wish to detect deception. If they can be engaged in a general conversation unrelated to the subject event prior to the interview this is ideal for helping to establish a baseline for both verbal and non-verbal behavior. In personal matters with family or friends, you have probably talked to them thousands of times. However, have you ever really paid attention to their personal verbal patterns? If not, do so before you broach a sensitive subject.

### The two memory centers of the brain
1.Memory records events along with all kinds of miscellaneous information it relates to a specific event. The mind will record miscellaneous information such as they were cold and standing in a water puddle when they saw the person shot. This miscellaneous information is generally something experienced by one of the senses **other than sight** such as taste or smell. What they felt about observing the event is also generally a

characteristic of a real memory. Please note that recounting this extraneous information is indicative of the truth, or a real memory, versus a constructed memory. When a memory is constructed it is almost always completely a recounting of what one would have seen if they observed the event.

2.The "Spell Checker" or "Filter" in our brain decides what information is verbalized. The language used to describe memory versus constructed stories or lies is different. True memory will throw in irrelevant information that does not directly relate to the subject event. So when in the subject provides an open statement, or the "initial" version, they will relate extraneous information such as how they felt or I was cold and standing in a puddle of water when I saw the shooting. If the only information related is strictly visual this is quite possibly an indicator of deception. If there is not any extraneous information in the initial version of the story you can ask them to elaborate about anything else they remember about the event. If they still do not relate any extraneous information it would be a fairly strong indicator of deception. Again this goes to a person's verbal patterns. Individuals trained to observe, such as police officers, may display this characteristic, and it would not necessarily be indicative of deception.

Start with 100% belief in the individual.
Try to understand what the subject is saying with the assumption that what he said is the truth. Remember they will try to tell you the truth even if they lead you to an incorrect conclusion by what they haven't said.

Ask Two questions of what was said.
"Why did the subject say it?" Was it important to the subject? Was it important to the story? Would it make them look

innocent? Think about all the possible ramifications of a statement not just the story told by the words.

"Why did the subject say it that way?" Did it tend to imply something not said? Did the wording depersonalize the victim? Could they have told it in a more direct manner? Could they have told it in a shorter way? Did it fit in the story at that point in time?

## Language Indicators of Deception

### First Person Past Tense
First person past tense notes ownership of the story. If it is a real memory the story will almost always be in first person past tense. Any other verbiage is indicative of a problem. Dropping the pronoun "I" is the first way individuals move away from first person past tense. When you start seeing statements such as "Woke up, got dressed, etc. without the "I" there is no commitment to what is being said. The more "I" is left out of a story the higher the probability the story is concocted. If "I" is only left out in certain places, focus on those areas for further questioning.

In the illustration above the subject has not committed to the fact that he went to the bar or the movies; he only committed to going home at some point.

Future Tense - Example: **I would never hurt her.** This is a common place, real world example of when a guilty person was asked about killing their spouse. The key here is that this in the future tense. He can't hurt her in the future, she is already dead. Note: he did not say he had not hurt or killed her. It is also important to note that he did not use her name or their relationship. The use of "her" versus her name or relationship helps them to de-personalize the situation. In the "initial" version, an innocent person would more likely say, "I did not kill my wife." Note "I" is used and the statement is in first person past tense.

I think, I believe
Think/believe (NO commitment) – Example: I think she was fine when I left for work. She was in the bedroom. There is no commitment to her being fine she may well have been dead in the bedroom from this statement.

Started and Other Edit Indicators
Started/began/proceeded/finished/continued/proceeded – These

words are keys that some information has been edited out of the story either intentionally or unintentionally.  It may be important or not.  You will want to ask follow-up questions such as "what were you doing just before you started."

### Remember
Remember – When the subject states "I remember" the statement that follows is important to the individual.  It may not turn out to be important to the investigation, but special attention should be given to it because it is important to the subject.

### Extraneous Information
Unimportant unnecessary information is indicative of real memory.  Example:  When I found her in the alley I felt like I was going to throw up.  I can't forget that smell and how she looked.  Note the subject is using first person past tense and the miscellaneous information is from real memory and indicative that the subject is telling the truth in this specific instance.  This only covers this specific instance, it does not mean the subject did not kill the victim several days earlier and later return to the scene and experience these emotions and record these memories.

### Social introduction
Order of appearance = priority

The order in which an individual introduces others not previously known to you or the interviewer is indicative of their priority to them at that moment in time and probably in general.  If the subject introduces another before his spouse that individual is more than likely more important to the subject at that moment in time than their spouse.  Remember this basically relates to social introductions and not necessarily in response to a direct question about a specific individual.

### Rate of speech
Slow: Carefully weighing each word to avoid a mistake. This is generally a significant indicator that the person is being deceptive or has something to hide they do not want to mistakenly disclose. Again remember the baseline on how a person normally speaks. If they always talk slowly and methodically it would not be an indication of deception.

Rapid nervousness: This is often an indication of a rehearsed story they are trying to get out before they forget something. After they finish rapidly telling a story ask them to start over from the end and go backwards. Tell them you need to make sure you got everything if they push for why. If they are being deceptive, they will generally make a detectable mistake in their second statement or narration of events in reverse.

### Unnecessary connections
After/left (skipped part of the story) If they throw in unnecessary connections, it is indicative that they have left out part of the story. It may or may not be consequential or intentional. After allowing them to finish the statement, ask them what happened immediately before or after the unnecessary connection. You may have to pursue this a little with additional questions.

### Looping
Going over a main point several times. When a person goes over a main point, several times on their own, without prodding; they are generally trying to convince you of their version of the story. A person who is telling the truth generally assumes it is the truth so I don't have to repeat or convince you that it is the truth.

# Rules for the Detailed Interview

## Rule 1
Information that comes as an answer to a specific question is less reliable than information that comes without a question. When you ask a person about a specific act it presses them into lying if they believe the consequences for telling the truth are too high. A statement such as "Tell me about last night when Helen was killed," will produce far more truthful information than, "Did you kill Helen." If the subject killed Helen you have just forced them into telling a lie or being deceptive. There are ways to gain this admission later in an interrogation, but if you force them into this at this point it helps to fortify their resolve.

## Rule 2
Specific questions teach a person what is important, and how to lie to us. The less information that can be conveyed in your question the better. It is far better to use "Tell Statements." Tell me about Sue. Tell me about last night. Tell me about your relationship with Sue.

## Rule 3
It is not easy to lie; a person will try to tell the truth. I have reviewed numerous interviews where it was obvious that the subject's statements were true, but that they lead you to the wrong conclusion.

## Rule 4
A question must never begin with negative expectations. You must always expect an answer. You must **not** communicate by your attitude or words that you think the subject will lie to you in response to your question.

Maintain the formula of Question? Answer.

Broken record tactic – Make sure the question asked is answered. If you learn nothing else from this book, learn this. I have watched hundreds of interviews and I would be a rich man if I had a dollar for every time the question was asked, and not answered, but the interviewer went on to the next question. I have seen this particularly in interviews of and by politicians about sensitive issues. The subject will respond, but not answer the question. I have asked the same question over and over numerous times before receiving an actual response to the question asked. This is uncomfortable for some interviewers. If you are uncomfortable, change up how you ask the same question and ask it again later in the interview. A question where they evade providing an actual response is one you need them to answer. You can easily practice and learn this technique by watching interviews of politicians. Actually, that may be the best way to learn many of these techniques. Additionally, watch bureaucrats being interviewed before any congressional committee. You will almost always see many of the indicators of deception present in their responses; and the representative or senator almost never catches it.

Difficult question tactic – When you ask a difficult question, wait for the answer. I can't count the times I have seen an interviewer ask a difficult question and move on without an answer, because the subject did not immediately provide a response. Silence is your friend after you ask a question. Shut up and wait for a response. That is worth repeating "Shut up and wait for a response." Don't jump-in immediately if a response is slow to come. Look at them as if you are expecting more information. They will feel the need to fill the silence.

### Responses Indicative of Truth

Subject doesn't need time to think of the "correct answer."

Subject speak easily in general terms.

Subject gives a strong yes or no.

Subject is willing to be emphatic in their response.

A truthful subject may need time to calm down after being angry.

Subject provides concise to the point information.

Responds with what you want to know, requires minimal questioning.

### General Types of Deceptive Responses

This is probably the most important area for VERBAL CONTENT ANALYSIS. These items are the most easily detected and are strong indicators of deception. They may not be an indicator of guilt but will certainly generally indicate that the subject is concealing something that is sensitive to them.

1. Deflects to another issue. This is a way to get the interviewer off track and deflect the interview to another safer area for the subject.

Here is another example of deflecting.

Question: Were you with another woman last night?

Response: You are so jealous, don't you trust me? Why do we have to keep going through these jealous rages of yours.

Note: The subject both turned it around and tried put the interviewer on the defense and make it about the interviewer. In neither did the subject make a simple direct response to the question.

2.Doesn't answer the question asked. Often it will seem like an answer but it is not actually an answer.

The subject did not answer the question of where they were last night. She could have been anywhere on Tuesday night with this answer.

3.Repeats the question. Repeating the question is generally a stalling tactic to think how they want to respond. If the question was particularly long, complex, or confusing they may simply be trying to understand

it.

4.Answers with a question? Check out the illustration above again. She followed up the repeated question with another question. If the subject would not really know the reason for the question it may be nothing. If the subject knows why the officer is asking it is a delaying technique to try and think up a plausible answer. Remember it may only be something they are embarrassed about that they are trying to conceal.

5.Qualifies answers. Statements such "As I recall," preceding the answer does not signify commitment to their answer.

6. Calms quickly after demonstration of anger. Guilty people do not like to be out of control for fear of making a mistake and will quickly regain their composure.

7. Needs time to think of the "best answer". Truthful people either know an answer to a question or don't and will respond relatively quickly. If you are wondering when they are going to respond, they are probably trying to think up the best answer to your question that will not implicate them or make them disclose something they do not wish to disclose. This does not hold true if you are asking about a long past event. However, a significant recent event will be easily and quickly recalled by a truthful individual.

8. Seeks more information from you about what you know as you are interviewing them. If they start asking questions of you, be extremely cautious that you do not disclose any information to them.

9. Liars lie specifically – They will tell you a truth that will lead you to an incorrect conclusion.

Note: He told the truth, to part of the question. Watch asking double questions such as this, they help the subject deliver a deceptive response.

### Religious Statements/Oaths
These statements are so often an indication of deception that I almost laugh when I hear them now. There are people that use some of these sayings regularly in their normal speech, but they are view and far between. Remember to check their baseline verbal responses before making an assumption. Truthful people generally do not feel a need to enlist statements such as these to make people believe them. In virtually every confession I ever obtained over the years at least at one or more one of these statements or a variation of one of the statements was used by the
suspect.

Honest to God

If there is a creator in heaven

As God is my witness

A God fearing person like myself

I swear on my mother's grave

May my parents drop dead

I'll swear on a stack of Bibles

I am a deacon in my church

## "NO" is important

How an individual says the word "NO" can be very telling. The following are examples of "No" that are indicative of deception.

A qualified "No" that answers only half the question.

Multiple "NOs" given in response to a single question.

If their "NO" is long and drawn out, say 3-5 seconds.

If they delay in saving "No" when other responses are timely.

If "NO" is stated too quickly, possibly before the question is even finished.

The subject sounds like he is out of breath when the responds "NO."

If a subject chuckles or laughs as they are stating "No" or after stating "No."


## False Issues

1. Want to engage in an argument over inconsequential irrelevant issues.

2. Past treatment – Examples:

The police have always harassed me needlessly.

You have never trusted me.

3. Unjustified anger over minor questions.

Question: Did you enjoy yourself at the party?

Response: What do you mean by that?

### Soft Words

The subject responds in a very low voice that you can barely hear. This is an extremely sensitive area for the subject, make sure you hear what they are saying and follow up. It is important to remember to model your tone and volume to the subjects tone and volume at this point. Modeling will be discussed further in the NON-VERBAL BEHAVIOR ANALYSIS section.

### Important Non-verbal Utterances

1. Whew -Glad it's over – Why would you say something like that unless you were under stress? You are generally under stress when you are trying to conceal something or be deceptive.

2. Sigh -Self-pity – Why would someone be feeling sorry for themselves if someone else is the victim. Be sensitive here, it could be a sense of loss if the subject was close to the victim.

3. Nervous Laugh -Fear – Subjects being interviewed are generally not given to be jovial in an interview setting. Nervous laughter can be a stress release.

### Lapses in Memory

Memory issues that are indicative of deception. This **does** relate to how recent an event was and the significance of the event. If it was a significant event the subject should recall it, even if a fairly long period of time has passed. The subject should remember at least the basic details of a significant event, and more with questioning. If the event would have been considered inconsequential to them, even fairly recent events may not be remembered. This does not relate to how observant a person is.

Remarkably good memory is a sign of rehearsal. Remember to see if they include miscellaneous unnecessary details, emotions felt, and sensory details such as smells or temperature.

Blackout – Very few people actually blackout. Check to see if they have a history of blackouts or a medical condition that may cause a blackout.

Memory failure cop- outs, bail outs

I don't think so

I can't recall

I can't remember

Not that I can think of

Not that I can remember

### Expressions Indicative of Guilt

These expressions are generally indicative of deception for the statement that accompanies the statement. Remember to check for the use of these expressions when obtaining the baseline. A fair amount of people use a portion of these expressions as part of their normal vocabulary. Be extra careful in establishing your baseline for the use of these statements. In personal matters you will generally know if a friend or family commonly uses any of these expressions.

"This is going to sound like a lie..,"  (This is going to be a lie.)

"I know you think that I'm lying, but..." (I am lying.)

"I couldn't lie to you..." (I am going to lie to you.)

"I have absolutely no reason to lie..." (I have lots of reason to lie to you.)

"You may not believe this, but..." (You shouldn't believe this.)

"To be honest..." (I am not going to be completely honest with you.)

"Honestly..." (The next statement is questionable. Be careful with this one since a fair amount of people use this in their normal speech patterns.)

"To clarify what I've been saying..." (Let me confuse you because you may have understood too much of what I was trying to conceal.)

"You may not believe anything else I've told you, but you must believe this!" (Because I don't want to go to jail)

"I'm not trying to evade the question, but..." (I am trying to evade the question.)

"I don't want to confuse you, but..." (I will try my best to confuse you and the issue.)

"To tell you the truth..." (I am not going to tell you the truth.)

"To answer that completely.,." (I am going to leave something out.)

"Well, frankly..." (I am not going to be completely truthful.)

"I know that this sounds strange, but..." (That's because I just made it up.)

"You're going to find this hard to believe, but..." (I know you are not going to buy this lie but I am going to try it anyway.)

## Camouflage Statements

Camouflage statements indicate that what the subject is about to talk about, is the most important to them. It may or may not be important to the investigation, but it is extremely important to them so pay close attention.

"By the way"

"Incidentally"

## Stalling and blocking methods

The subject will use these methods to help them avoid answering a question or to give them time to think up a plausible answer.

Subject asks you to repeat the question. (They are trying to think of the best answer that will be believable and not incriminate them. If you asked a long convoluted question this does not apply. I have generally seen the convoluted question more with attorneys than investigators.)

Subject repeats the question before he answers it. (Gives the subject time to think up an answer.)

Subject states that he has already answered that question. (They are trying to get out of answering the question. They will use this one often when you are using the broken record technique to try and get an answer to a question they never really answer.)

Subject states "Like I told you before" (Subject will generally repeat the previous non-answer they provided to the question. Use the broken record technique with the explanation that their response did not really answer the question.)

## Guilt signatures

These are strong indicators that the subject is guilty of the incident in question. If you get a subject to this point you may want to progress into the interrogation to attempt to obtain a full confession. When you see these statements the subject is generally feeling guilty and it is a good indicator that a confession is obtainable.

"I am not that type person"- This is a strong indicator of guilt where the issue is a moral issue. They are not saying they did not commit the act, but that they do not see themselves as the type of person that would commit such an act. While it may be repugnant to you, the more you can help the subject rationalize that the act as acceptable or someone else's fault the more likely you are to obtain a confession.

Subject talks about past troubles, particularly those of a similar nature.

Admission of something they did wrong in the past that is similar. Example: Rape suspect. I know I was convicted of rape before, but that is all behind me.

Agrees that they look guilty.

Strong denial to virtually everything – (They do not want to be associated with the event in any way even though they obviously have some connection to the event. An innocent person will generally tell you about any connection he had to the victim or the event in question.)

Accuses the interviewer of prejudice against them; and of already making up their mind.

## Closing the interview

Story reversal- Get them to go through the story from end to beginning. This will often illustrate discrepancies.

Split-reversal – start in the middle and go to the start and then jump to the end and move back to the middle. Again this will often illustrate discrepancies.

Have the subject repeat important assertions made during the course of the interview. Particularly, things you know to be false. Get them to commit to any lies they have told and any important assertions. This will be important both in any interrogation phase and for later in any court proceedings when they change their story. You can use these statements in a court to impeach them if they lie.

If you do not plan to immediately proceed into an interrogation leave the door open for future contact for additional questions. Even if you proceed into an interrogation attempt to leave the door open for further questions.

## Non-verbal Behavior Analysis (NBA)

Non-Verbal Behavior Analysis is the science of studying human movement, especially when combined with verbal statements. You will often hear this referred to as body language. Body language depends on the proximity of the interviewer to the subject being interviewed. Remember you need a baseline to establish a norm. In a formal interview you will accomplish this by asking various non-confrontational questions to which you know the answers. Request information such as their name, address, marital status, where they work, and what kind of car they drive. You should modify and not use any of these questions that might be pertinent to the investigation. After you have used this to establish a baseline, you can start the actual formal part of the interview. Note: There are many similarities to VERBAL CONTENT ANALYSIS. However, I will cover the recommendations for using NON-VERBAL BEHAVIOR ANALYSIS so that you can select how to compromise on the areas of conflict. The choice of how to combine the two methods depends on the personality of the interviewer.

When you are attempting to use NON-VERBAL BEHAVIOR ANALYSIS in an informal setting, try to engage the subject in a conversation about themselves. If you show interest in a person and their life, they will almost always start telling you about themselves. Everyone loves to talk about themselves, if given the opportunity. If they fail to talk about themselves and are not shy by nature, this is a cause for concern about whether their responses can be used as a baseline for their normal truthful behavior. If they talk freely about themselves when you show interest, their responses will generally provide a good baseline for identifying when they are being truthful. Remember for NON-VERBAL BEHAVIOR ANALYSIS you are trying to observe their body and how it reacts to different stimuli.

## The Interview

### The Interview Setting
For NON-VERBAL BEHAVIOR ANALYSIS to be most effective you need to be within an individual's private or intimate zone. Generally for Americans the private zone is about five feet while the intimate zone is about three feet. You must at least be within

the private zone and it is preferable to be within the intimate zone. The intimate zone varies by person, and particularly by nationality. The intimate zone for many other nationalities is much closer, often within twelve inches. This can be determined by observing how close they get to someone they know when they are having a conversation. To be truly effective you must be within that intimate zone, even if it is not comfortable for you. The first time I interviewed someone with a private zone of less than a foot they backed me across the room before I realized that they expected to be that close, to engage in a personal conversation.

The ideal situation is to be:

-seated within three feet with nothing between you;

-in a private area (preferably with no windows visible to them where activity might distract them);

-Uninterrupted (Make sure to the extent possible that you will not be interrupted by others).

### Interviewer attitude

The interviewer's attitude is paramount to success. Starting out as an angry accusatory interviewer will not bring success. If you cannot bring yourself to portray the following traits you need to allow someone else to conduct the interview. Alternatively wait until such time as you can calmly conduct the interview. You must start the interview with the following techniques and attitudes on display. Latter after you have gathered adequate information the techniques may shift to an interrogation mode, if appropriate.

Interested- You not only should seem to be genuinely interested in the subject's version of the story, but truly interested. How they tell the story and their accompanying physical response are the key to detecting deception with this technique. Their physical response needs to be determined in conjunction with the response to a question.

Sincere – You cannot display skepticism or disbelief in the subject.

Understanding – Whether you understand why they took certain actions or not you must indicate an understanding. Allowing a subject to rationalize their behavior is often key to obtaining their confession. This is often one of the most difficult tasks for an interviewer. You may well have to indicate acceptance and understanding of an act you consider repulsive. This is particularly true where you have minimal evidence, and conviction may well rest on whether a confession is obtained.

Objective – You have to start out objectively and not with an accusatory tone. If you are accusatory it will put the subject on notice to exercise care with his answers. In a public setting, this means engaging the subject to talk about their self in a low key manner. Slowly work around to the subject of your interest.

Even Tempered – You must control your temper. If it is plain that you are mad or upset the subject will be on the defensive and it will negatively affect your ability to detect NON-VERBAL BEHAVIOR ANALYSIS indicators.

Polite – Virtually all people respond well to being treated politely and with respect. As an investigator I always found that this worked to my benefit in the interview process. Surprisingly, it had a more positive affect on those who were used to being treated harshly, because of their poor choices, such as habitual drunkards and drug users. While you will want to be polite to someone accustomed to being treated with deference, you will want to gain control by using their first name, and don't be overly accommodating. All though playing a little dense can often help acquire information with someone who is self-important and considers that they are above being questioned.

### Interviewer tone
Volume - A low quiet tone conveys privacy. You will be astonished at how this one thing can affect an interview. Lower your voice, not to a whisper, but a quiet tone like you would use in a crowded area where you did not want anyone else to overhear you talking to a friend.

Conversational Tone— The tone should be easy going and friendly almost like you were talking to a friend. You are attempting to develop a bond of trust.

Display No skepticism- Skepticism puts them on defense. The one exception might be when a statement is so outlandishly unbelievable that the subject would not expect you to accept it on face value.

### Modeling
Individuals are most comfortable with those that they perceive to be like them. If you are too obvious about modeling any aspect of their behavior it will generally backfire on you, so be careful in using this technique.

**Don't take the modeling too far, it will backfire.**

Posture -This can be done by assuming a similar posture to that of the subject. Don't be obvious about this.

Voice tone- Don't do this unless you can do it effectively. If the subject perceives that you are mimicking them they will think you are mocking or making fun of them.

Pace of speech- If the person talks slow, slow down and keep a similar pace. Do the same if they talk fast, within reason. Again move slowly into this and do not make it obvious.

Language- Try to adapt the vocabulary level to the subject's. Don't use big unusual or complex words with a subject. The exception is, unless that is something it is obvious the subject is comfortable with and uses in their normal speech pattern. I have seen interviews of street people where the subject did not have a clue what the investigator was talking about.  The subjects did not have a clue what some of the words used by the investigator meant.

Encourage the subject to continue talking – Nods of ascent and simple acknowledgements will generally keep a subject talking.  Don't rush to fill the silence.

Let the subject know you are listening.  Nod attentively, make eye contact, mumble ascent where appropriate.  NEVER EVER INTERRUPT the subject while they are still talking.  This includes even if they are off on a rambling discourse.  When they stop talking steer them back around to the question, if it was not answered.  (This does not necessarily apply to a subject you are certain has a mental disability.)

Controlled silence. (shut-up and let them talk) After you ask a question, the subject will often give a very short response.  Don't immediately start talking or asking another question.  Be silent and see if they will elaborate more.  This is quite effective because people are uncomfortable with silence.

Don't interrupt the subject, use short expressions of interest.

-Amusement

-Sympathy

-Empathy

-Surprise

## Note Taking

Note Taking is permissible during the gathering of personal data in a formal interview. If it is not a formal interview and investigation, you will want to avoid taking notes. Regardless, always show interest in the subject's words and statements.

Note taking is NOT permitted during the story phase of the interview. The exception is writing down dates, addresses, telephone numbers, etc. When you ask the subject to tell you what happened regarding the event that is the subject of the investigation, listen closely. I highly recommend that the interview be video recorded for several reasons.

1.-You will want to go back over it for information that you missed. It is almost impossible to catch everything during the interview because you will often have to formulate the next question. While you want a list of questions to make sure you cover everything you have to pay sufficient attention to follow up on information discovered in the course of the interview. I have seen investigators loose valuable information because they struck strictly to their list of questions and did not follow up on the subject's responses. Additionally, you will catch NON-VERBAL BEHAVIOR ANALYSIS indicators that you missed during the course of the interview.

2.-If there is any possibility of legal action, criminal or civil, you will want the recording to corroborate the statements made in the interview. Without a recording it will simply be a he said she said argument. If you anticipate legal action I suggest you review evidentiary procedures. If you make the recording and secure the recording and can testify to the authenticity and that it has not been modified, you will probably be able to get it admitted into evidence. It can also protect you from allegations of misconduct in the interview. Additionally, I often use the recording to develop a written statement for the subject to sign in front of a notary at a later date. This would remove any argument that the subject was under duress to sign the statement.

3.-The final reason is to learn from your errors in the interview. I have never listened to one of my interviews where I did not hear something that I realized I should have followed up on more.

### Face to face interviews
While you think you are interviewing or questioning someone, that is just half the story. Every question you ask the subject, teaches them what you are interested in. Inexperienced and experienced investigators will often give more information away than they obtain. You will often see examples of this on TV. The investigator tells the whole story and then asks a simple yes, no question, and the interview is over. The investigator does not really gain any information from the subject, but has told the subject a significant part of the story. The interview also teaches the subject what is important to the interviewer. It teaches the subject what to lie about if they have something to hide.

## NON-VERBAL BEHAVIOR ANALYSIS Indicators

### The Eyes:
Recent studies have shown that even fairly experienced interviewers are generally only moderately successful at correctly interpreting eye movements. Interviewers have been much more successful at correctly applying other Non-verbal indicators. However, because the eye movements have been taught for years they are included here for reference. It is highly recommended that you concentrate on other Non-Verbal Indicators to assist in detecting deception.

The face and the eyes are considered by many to be the most expressive part of the human body.  They are the hardest to control and can display a variety of emotional responses.

There are a number of studies involving eye movement and a variety of opinions on the meanings of the movement.  Generally, for most of the population the consensus of many studies is that the following eye movements are correlated to the following emotions.

1.-HIGH LEFT = Visual Memory (Their left, your right) The general consensus is that when an individual is looking high and to their left they are recalling visual facts from memory.

2.-LEFT =Auditory Memory (Their left, your right) The general consensus is that when an individual is looking to their left they are recalling auditory facts from memory.

3.-HIGH RIGHT = Visual Construction (Their right, your left.) The general consensus is that when someone is looking high and to the right they are constructing a visual scenario and not recalling an event from memory.

4.-RIGHT = Auditory Construction (Their right, your left.) The general consensus is that when someone is looking to the right they are constructing an auditory scenario and not recalling an event from memory. For our purposes if the subject looks to their right they are making up a tory to tell us.

Develop a Baseline

1.-Before using these, develop a norm for the individual being interviewed. While asking biographical questions to which you expect an honest answer observe the eyes. Most will look high left when searching memory.

2.-Ask the subject a question you expect them to lie about.
    Have you ever lied to get out of trouble?

3.-Have you ever stolen anything?

4.-Most people will look high right, construction if they answer "No.".

5.-If the person looks straight ahead in an unfocused way they are probably in memory.

6.-When someone has answered the same question in the recent past they may look straight to the left recalling what they said before.


These are the most common and predictable patterns of eye movement. REMEMBER THERE ARE NO HARD AND FAST RULES. WATCH THE SUBJECT AND DETERMINE WHAT NORMAL IS FOR THEM.

Cautions:

I personally do not use this method due to the difficulty in observing the eye movements while making other observations and asking questions. Additionally, recent studies of this method utilizing experienced investigators were successful only about 50-

60% percent of the time.

These directions may well be reversed for a left handed person.

If the subject has severe mental or emotional problems, or possibly an antisocial personality; they may display a marked lack of emotion in the eyes and very little eye movement, i.e. a flat stare.

If you are in the private or intimate zone and you see the whites of their eyes, on both sides and bottom, back up, they are under extreme stress. Their actions are unpredictable.

Don't forget, a significant number of guilty people can look you in the eye just like an innocent person.

### The Rest of the Body.

Lying produces stress. Stress shows up in a number of body movements. Some of these may be grooming gestures by the subject. The more the subject can be observed the more you will understand these gestures. You need to develop a baseline for the subject's normal behavior. The higher the stakes are, the more reliable the indicators. Indicators are more reliable when read in groups.

Similar to the human eye, each body movement is associated with underlying emotional triggers. If you're able to learn body language, you'll have a better understanding of their emotional state. The subject won't understand they are giving themself away simply by making certain body movements. The body movements are just about all, executed unconsciously. The unconscious mind actually controls a significant part of a person's actions without their awareness. Many of the movements related to an individual's emotional state are orchestrated by their unconscious thoughts.

Understanding exactly what each body movement generally signifies is very important. In observing another person's body language, you will generally be able to determine their emotional state and whether it indicates that the individual is lying, or stating the truth. Here are some of the most typical characteristics of a subject who is lying or being deceptive. Remember observing the individual prior to the interview to develop a baseline is critical to accurate interpretation of body movements.

### Deceptive Body Language Indicators

New studies indicate body language is one of the more reliable types of indicators. When a subject is lying or being deceptive their actual physical movements in their arms and hands will decrease significantly. In other words if you have someone who talks with their hands, who suddenly stops using them or uses them minimally, they are probably constructing a story, a lie.

If he goes from this, to this.
It is a very good indicator of deception.

Major body movements may be observed in conjunction with the lie to relieve the stress. What I have generally observed is that when they lie about the most significant part of the story they will uncross their legs and re-cross them in the opposite direction. They may alternately shift significantly in the chair sitting up, slumping, or changing orientation from left to right or vice versa.

Touching the nose, face, or ears is a good indicator of stress if there are no physical causes. The touch will be more of a light touch that might hide the mouth and generally not a vigorous motion such as scratching.

Stroking or touching a mustache may be stress or a grooming behavior. If it tends to hide the mouth while they are talking they are probably uncomfortable with what they are saying. This may be an indicator of deception or depending on the person an embarrassing subject.

A dry mouth or lips is a good indicator of stress. Licking ones lips right after stating something may be an indication of deception. Whenever, individuals get anxious, their mouths become dry. There are actually a couple of explanations why an individual might possibly lick their lips immediately after stating something. They're either anxious, or are actually uncomfortable with what they just stated.

A lot of smiling is also an indicator of stress. Generally, people are not going to smile a lot in a formal interview.

A sudden onset of facial tics, stuttering or serious muscle spasms in their arms or legs is a good indicator of guilt. I have actually had an individual become so nervous when we got to the critical part of the interview that he almost could not talk because he started stuttering so violently. He did not have that issue before or after the crucial questions of guilt where he was able to tell the truth.

The sudden onset of flushing in the upper chest, neck and face indicates stress.

Adjusting or playing with jewelry, clothing, and glasses may indicate stress. It may also be a grooming gesture. Be particularly careful of this because a lot of people have nervous grooming habits such as spinning a ring on their finger.

Watch for the verbal response and the body movement to disagree. i.e. nodding yes while saying no or vice versa. This is usually an unconscious movement; it signifies they don't believe in what they just stated. The body movement is generally the truth about the question.

When an individual crosses their arms at a particular point in an interview it is probably a defensive gesture. If you observe carefully the time, place, and duration of the arms being crossed you can usually determine if this is a defensive gesture or simply a resting posture that is normal for the subject.

If the subject crosses both his arms and legs at the same time during the course of the interview this is probably a defensive gesture.  If it occurs at the point a critical question is being asked it is probably both a defensive gesture and a method to release stress.

Generally a subject's palms will probably face down whenever they are lying, since the unconscious mind believes you are more vulnerable whenever your palms are face up.

In some instances, they may avoid eye contact. There may also be various other explanations as to why they may be avoiding eye contact. Some individuals could have social disabilities, or it could possibly be they are simply looking at something. Additional factors could possibly be cultural, or an individual is self-conscious. You need to consider these aspects before you make a judgment.  If the subject usually maintains eye contact and all of a sudden they stop, it should be somewhat suspect.

Always, I repeat always, take into consideration their baseline behavior. Remember to read these patterns in groups.  One body language indicator may arouse suspicion but remember it is far preferable to read them in groups of 3-4.  Where in the interview the indicator occurs is also significant.  If it occurs near critical questions, it is far more significant than if it occurs during basic fact gathering, such as name and address.

Are they being deceptive?
Let's review some of the examples from the introduction and now see if you can tell when the subject is being deceptive. Remember to combine both verbal content analysis and non-verbal behavior analysis in making your determination. The illustration can't show the non-verbal behavior as well but I did try to work it in.  I placed the analysis of each illustration after all of the illustrations to give you the opportunity to develop your skills.

Skill Review and Practice

Here are the original illustrations from the introduction. If you didn't originally mark whether you thought the subject was being truthful, lying, or being deceptive, please do so now. We will now go over each illustrated scenario. Please check our analysis against your own analysis.

> Did you go to Bob's house last night?

> I went to Jane's house last night.

I am shocked this teen is being deceptive. There is not really a lot wrong with the mother's question. However, the question was not answered. You would expect a "NO" if the teen was being honest. Next you would use the broken record tactic. The teen would most likely slip into deflection mode indicating that you don't trust her or why do you need to know all of her business.

The first problem is with the question. This easily helps them determine what your interest and suspicions are. That information will put the subject on the defensive. This question might be appropriate later in the process. Better to gather information first about where they were when the incident occurred and other relevant information. The subject has avoided a simple "NO" statement which is how most innocent people would have responded. An innocent person would be fairly emphatic and might even be angered that you asked. The subject is using a future tense. He would be telling the truth now because he certainly cannot harm Joe since he is already dead. The subject has avoided using the first person past tense.

> **Did you go to the bar last night?**
>
> **Did I go to the bar last night? Why would you ask such a thing? YOU HAVE NEVER TRUSTED ME!**

This subject illustrates many of the indicators of deception. First he repeats the question to give him time to respond. Then he asks a question instead of responding. Then he deflects it so that the problem is that the female doesn't trust him instead of simply answering that he did or did not go to the bar last night. In a formal investigation you probably would have wanted to first ask the question "Where did you go last night?" Then you have them committed to a story before you make any type of accusation.

**Did you rob the store and shoot the clerk?**

*Didn't shoot the clerk.*

First the question is a problem because it asks a double question and is accusatory in nature. It would be better to gather other facts first. The subject is being deceptive in at least two ways. First he has avoided using the first person past tense. Second he qualified his answer that he did not shoot the clerk. Remember liars lie specifically. He may have participated in the robbery but not shooting the clerk although there was no real commitment to that because he did not use first person past tense.

We have previously discussed how this question was asked above. This subject is probably being truthful. He has used an inclusive statement emphatically without hesitation or qualifiers.

# Summary

Remember to always establish a baseline of behavior whether using Non-Verbal Indicators or Verbal Content Analysis. Be sure to look at the totality of the circumstances and to make a judgment judiciously. These techniques have helped me to uncover lies and obtain confessions in numerous cases. I am sure you will have similar success if you study the techniques and practice them with care.

## About the Author

*Mark Menefee is part of the baby boom generation. He was born in Abilene, Texas, in the early 1950's. Mark graduated from Texas A&M University with a BBA in accounting. After having served as an analyst in the US Air Force and a police officer in Bryan, TX, he spent many years running his own business before returning to public service. He spent many years working for the State of Texas in various investigative positions. After 20 plus years as a fraud investigator, he retired from the State. Based on his many years of experience and training he came to recognize verbal and body language indicative of deception. He has articulated those indicators in his book "Easy Lie Detection.*

Printed in Great Britain
by Amazon